So Inspired:
Preludes & Poems
For All People

So Inspired:
Preludes & Poems

For All People

JERRY BROWN SCHWARTZ

Illustrated by Michael Van Tonder

www.ivyhousebooks.com

Dedicated to my rare, delightful husband Harry, who makes waking up each day a special joy, and who believes in all my endeavors either big or small, and encourages me each day to pursue these as goals. This book is one of those goals.

PUBLISHED BY IVY HOUSE PUBLISHING GROUP
5122 Bur Oak Circle, Raleigh, NC 27612
United States of America
919-782-0281
www.ivyhousebooks.com

ISBN13: 978-1-57197-494-5
Library of Congress Control Number: 2008943165

Printed in the United States of America

Contents

About the Author

The richness of diverse experiences, from life in the tranquil rural South to the busy bustle of New York City, have been the seeds of Jerry Brown Schwartz's life lessons and the inspiration for her poetry.

Schwartz grew up on a farm in Smyrna, Georgia, where the surrounding forests and creeks served as a playground for her and her five siblings. In this simple chapter of her life, front porch storytelling sessions, rhyme writing, thought-provoking books, and adventures in nature, fueled her imagination.

Through the years, Schwartz maintained her love for the written word and Mother Nature. In retirement, with her husband Harry's encouragement, she picked up her pen, as well as her gardening gloves, once again. She continues to infuse her writing with verbal snapshots taken from her homes in the mountains of North Carolina and Georgia, as well as sunny Florida.

Preface

My preludes are the inspirations for my poetry. A few of the people's names have been changed, but all are real; the places, pets and experiences have given and continue to give my life inspiration. I am thankful for growing up on a farm, and to my mama and daddy. Mama gave me her city heart and ornery ways. Daddy gave me his gentleness and the love of the outdoors. He taught me to start each day as if something very special is going to happen, and about the glorious and healing quality of laughter and activity in life each day. I am thankful for knowing the taste of homemade peach ice-cream eaten Sunday afternoons on the front porch with the family, so delicious that your tongue danced and shivered as it touched each taste bud. I thank my brothers and sisters for the fun, sharing and knowing the security that someone was there to watch your back.

"Everything which I have created as a poet has had its origin in a frame of mind and a situation in life, I never wrote because I had, as they say, found a good subject."

—HENRIK JOHAN IBSEN
1828-1906
Norwegian Playwright

Winning Ways Prelude

After phoning a friend's mom and dad, to wish them a happy anniversary, I felt somewhat lonely for my own mama and daddy, who have been in heaven more than ten years.

Although I had never met my friend's parents, the conversation flowed freely, evoking feelings that I had as a child when I listened to my beautiful mama talk with neighbors on our visits. Sooner or later, mama always ended up talking about her favorite subject—flowers.

Her dad ended our talk saying, "When my daughter visits, I will send you some surprise lilies." I am grateful to them for inspiring this dearest memory of my mama.

Mama always named her different gardens. The tomato garden was called the Red Garden; the beets, carrots, turnips, yams and onions grew in the Dig Em Up Soon Garden, and the jonquils, crocuses, and plum trees grew in the Open Season Garden. My favorite garden, by far the most beautiful, was the Winning Ways Garden. A few years before mama went to heaven at age eighty two, she told me how the Winning Ways Garden came about.

Mama had taken us, her six children, on one of her numerous visits to a neighbor. We always had our little red wagon, which carried a few rolled up feed sacks and a few indispensable garden tools in tow. The tools were put to use helping our neighbors with chores, or just in case we had to dig up a few gifts of flowers.

After one of these particular visits, as we sallied forth with our red wagon stacked high with flower cuttings, bulbs and seeds, our neighbor said, with a twinkle in his eye, "Mrs. Brown, you sure have winning ways."

So inspired . . . "Winning Ways."

Winning Ways

It was our mama's way
To visit with a neighbor
And linger half the day.

Talk would be satisfied
About all the neighbors and each child;
We would sit and smile
Listening all the while.

Each visit was surely to end
With flowers and woody plants;
Our mama's winning way
Left nothing to chance.

Mama was a master
With her winning ways;
When she would start her magic
This was what she had to say:

"Mr. Redden, we could move the yellow bells
The surprise lilies could see the sun
The children won't mind a bit, you know,
They do it all in fun."

Out would pop her pruning shears
And she would make a cut or two,
"Remember, Mr. Redden
I am doing this for you."

"The daisies and the liriope
Would grow better apart.
Let's see if we can give them
A better, fresh, new start.

"I've noticed that the irises are
A bit huddled together this year,
And those violet Johnny jump ups
Are the cutest little dears."

"The flowers could use some thinning;
The children are always willing.
To take on this small task
Is but a little thing to ask."

After gathering bulbs, cuttings and seeds,
And once mama had satisfied all her flower needs,
Back to our cozy farm we did go
Where we planted our gifts, and watched
them grow.

With each visit upon our neighbors
Their high regard for mama grew.
As each flower took its root,
Friendships with understanding mamma
did accrue.

Our beautiful mamma with the winning ways,
Dispatched her children to each neighboring place
To assist the neighbor with a needed chore.
That was the way she evened the score.

5

Jessie Teaches Tessie to Sing Prelude

Walking through my garden, I discovered a beautiful writing spider had blocked a pathway with an astonishing web. Her web looked like a big spun gossamer curtain, and she was center stage. Each time an insect flew into her web, she ran to her captive, tied it up, and ran back to center stage.

Since I am a bug lover, I thought, how nice if this spider would eat veggies instead of my gardens very necessary insects. So inspired . . . "Jessie Teaches Tessie to Sing."

Jessie Teaches Tessie to Sing

A wondrous, imaginative child named Jessie
Played in her mother's garden excessively.
She loved the birds, but favored the bugs impressively.

One day she befriended a clever writing
Spider named Tessie. Tessie wove an
Astonishing web to catch bugs flying by.
Both good and bad bugs she found delectable;
Her ravenous appetite demanded feeding
From morning into the night. Tessie stashed
Her captives, in the blink of an eye.

But a garden needs insects to pollinate for seeds.
If Tessie eats all of them, fruits and flowers won't be seen.

Seeing her mother's concern for her garden,
For the beautiful flowers of spring,
Jessie prayed that morning, asked God what to do,
Then ran to the garden to let Tessie know. "Tessie,"
Said Jessie, "I will teach you to sing, and
You can eat veggies instead of butterfly wings."

Tessie was talented and practiced each day.
She soon drew a crowd quite willing to pay.

Tessie now sings center stage on her web,
Has her meals delivered; carrots, turnips and greens.
Jessie is back in the garden befriending the bugs.
Her mother is happy, viewing the delightful scene
Of Tessie singing arias and enjoying her new cuisine.

Butterflies now dance and bees do their thing
When an aria Tessie begins to sing.

Who Needs A Falling Star Prelude

My grandmother Monty and I would sit on the front porch in the evenings watching for falling stars. A tale has it that, if you wish upon a falling star your wish will come true. For a poor child, this was very heartfelt.

We didn't see many falling stars, but this didn't discourage us from waiting patiently for these rare occurrences.

The one thing we did see lots of was "lightning bugs" or "fireflies." They twinkle in the darkness. A flash of light here, then there, created a magical setting for my grandmother and me as we sat in darkness on our beloved front porch with out cherished wishes and dreams.

My grandmother's eyesight was not the best. She would say, excitedly, "There sugar, over there, that's a falling star."

"No, Monty, that's a lightning bug," I would tell her. Not in the least deterred, she would say, "Well, let's make a wish anyway."

My grandmother and I spent many sweet evenings together in just this way. Both of us full of wishes to see the falling stars, and in the full belief that our wishes, blessed with a far off flash of light, would come true, and mine did.

So inspired . . . "Who Needs a Falling Star."

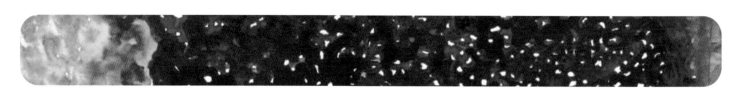

Who Needs A Falling Star

If you don't see a falling star
And a wish you're longing for
Wish upon a lightning bug
And your wish may well occur.

His light is blinking in the night
Not to light his path—¬
He's signaling for a special plight
To secure a mate for his delight

With so many lighting up the night
Who cares about no falling stars
Wish upon a lightning bug
For they are near and far

If the lightning bug flies higher
Your wish will then be granted
If the lightning bug flies earthward
Then your wish will be firmly planted

Tomorrow brings another night
Of dreams with peaceful slumber
Falling stars and lightning bugs
Are quietly waiting yonder

I'll just close my eyes and rest with ease.
"Mr. Lightning Bug, grant my wish, please."

Deception Prelude

My flower gardens are one of my spirit's celebrated pleasures. The gardens attract many fascinating insects, different types of bees, my favorite one—the honeybee—gathering pollen, knowing the many colors are there to entice them to call. The ever wonderful aphid eating lady bugs, the talented writing spiders, the beautiful gleaming blue dragon flies, a great hunter to the dismay of many insects; in turn, the many insects attract the lizards. As a friend and I were walking through the gardens, we stopped to watch the silhouette of a green lizard on a hosta leaf. She made the comment, "Lizards look quite intelligent." After our visit, I returned to the garden, sitting on my favorite rock bench because it has the best view to watch all the events happening with the animals and insects. I was continually drawn to the green salamander.

So inspired . . . "Deception."

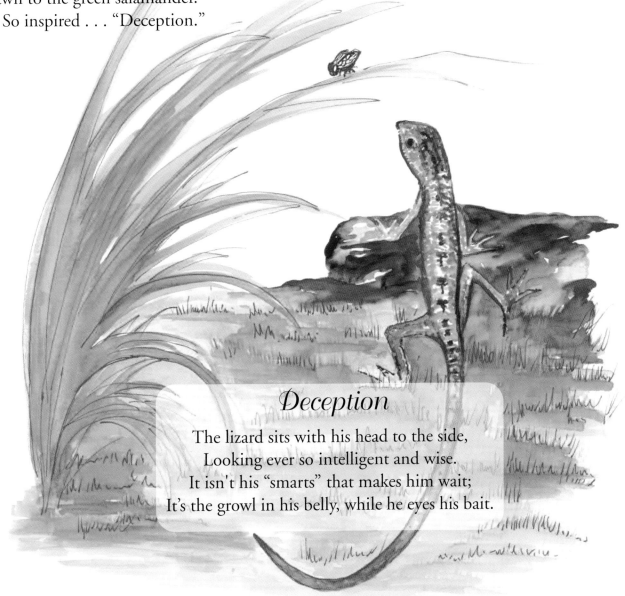

Deception

The lizard sits with his head to the side,
Looking ever so intelligent and wise.
It isn't his "smarts" that makes him wait;
It's the growl in his belly, while he eyes his bait.

Within the Forest Prelude

I have always loved to walk alone in the forest. Even if I sometimes feel apprehensive about being by myself, I overcome this feeling by becoming aware of the many mysteries that one can discover around each turn in the path.

On these walks all sense of time leaves me. Knowing that humans did not design this wonderment is enough to have me seeking hidden pathways in the forest.

So inspired . . . "Within the Forest."

Within the Forest

Within the forest
A path does stray
And beckons you
To walk its way

Within the forest
A creek does flow
Over the rocks
Smooth and slow

Within the forest
Mushrooms grow
Beside the ferns
Row upon row

Within the forest
A single wildflower
Nods at you
With majestic power

Within the forest
Sumac abides
And can make you itch
On your backside

Within the forest
A small pond waits
For a fisherman's pole
Alive with bait

Within the forest
A face you may see
On the old cedar tree
By letting your imagination
Roam quite free

Within the forest
Baby rabbits sleep
While baby birds
Above them peep

Within the forest
Squirrels and chipmunks scurry
As you walk by
In too big a hurry

Within the forest
Deer do stay
And watch for hunters
Then run away

Within the forest
A red hawk will light
To bring a message
For your insight

Within the forest
A soft rain shower falls
Soothing your head and heart
From hurtful recall

Within the forest
You'll find a sweet retreat
To return to
From life's burdens you meet

Within the forest
Your mind can rest
While renewing your soul
To be your best

Within the forest
Stop and rest awhile
Think back to the days
As a sleeping child

Within the forest
One can think
Then write it down
With pen and ink

Harry's Morning Walk Prelude

Harry and I have a home in a beautiful area of North Carolina called King Mountain. Each morning my husband takes a walk. When he returns, he describes the sights and sounds of his walk.

So inspired . . . "Harry's Morning Walk."

Harry's Morning Walk

King Mountain is magical
With wonders to see
There's always another walk
Waiting for thee

Head up the hill
King circle you'll make
Take off a few pounds
From late dinner and cake

Stroll by the remembrance
Tom made for Beau
Sit on a rock
And ponder the show

Watch a new neighbor
Building a home
Think about old friends
Who have up and gone

Meander along,
Swinging your arms,
Beside roadside gardens
Bursting with charm

Sit by the pond
Watch the trout play around
And just enjoy this life
Without making a sound

Meet the silver fox
Crossing the road
Is he seeking a handout?
Or maybe a toad?

Ponder the view
From George's bench
Sail on a cloud
That's within your reach

Smell the breeze
That floats from above
And dream about
The one you love

Watch the red tailed hawk
Sail through the valley
Then scoop for a rabbit
Right up his alley

Around the bend,
The home fires are burning
A walk on the mountain
Gets one's heart churning

Rock on your porch
With the mountains in view
So grateful to know
That you are one of the lucky few

A Questionable Tale Prelude

When I was a child, my mother told a story about an uncle whom we never actually met, but who was a very vivid character to us. While hoeing in his cornfield one day, my uncle encountered a snake. The snake chased him across a rather large cornfield. His bravery in outrunning the snake is the stuff of family legend. I accepted this tale as undisputed fact. Just the thought of being chased by a snake planted such fear in us that we honed our skills of escape on a regular basis. We often practiced outrunning our imaginary pursuer and we prided ourselves that we could outrun any snake that dared to take us on.

Every Sunday morning on our way to church, we took a shortcut across a field that had high grass growing for the cows. Mama would walk to the door and holler out at us, "Watch out for snakes in that field."

In all the years that we repeated this weekly ritual, we never came upon any bad snakes. Now and then we would see a little green snake or a king snake. Mama told us "to never harm king snakes because they kept the bad snakes and mice in check."

Mama's story was always in the back lobes of my memory. On a beautiful spring morning, I was deadheading some flowers in my garden, when I heard a terrified scream, "A snake is chasing me! Help!" I turned to see the girl, who was helping me with garden chores, running all out toward me, still screaming. Lo and behold, right behind her was a copperhead in hot pursuit. My nephew was working close by, and having heard all the commotion, came to her rescue and killed the poor snake with a hoe.

All those years later, mama's story about my uncle was validated at last—he was brave and fast. So inspired . . . "A Questionable Tale."

A Questionable Tale

Mr. John Roy, while on his way to church,
Came upon a king snake, which caused his heart to lurch.

Hoping for a friend, with some give and take
"Where are you going?" asked optimistic Mr. Snake.

"I am on my way to pray, I'll even say one for you today."

"I don't need a prayer because I have alchemy.
Come a little closer and maybe get to know me."

"Not me," said Mr. John Roy. "That may be a ploy,
I'll be off to church now and join the hoi polloi."

Mr. King snake raised his head,
"I am sorry you're afraid because you don't understand;
God gave me quite a purpose
When he put me on this land.
You may have ophidiophobia, but for this there is a cure.
Open your mind, investigate, you'll find an answer I'm sure.
I am a symbol of wisdom, expressed through doctor's healing,
So think of this, John Roy, while in your church you're kneeling."

Mr. King snake went on his way, feeling misunderstood.
He thought, "Mr. John Roy's head is about as hard as wood."

"I'll curl up under this rock, and have a warm peaceful night,
And say my prayer, for God to show a king snake a friendly knight."

Three Sisters Prelude

There were six children in my family: three boys and three girls. Our beautiful sister, Polly, with a generous heart, delicate voice, glorious hair, and a delight in each experience every blessed day, died at the age of fifty. This left an empty space in our lives. We feel it most at our family get togethers when someone says, "Let me take a picture of you five!"

We miss our beloved sister everyday. This poem about three sisters in no way reflects diminished love for my three brothers. All my brothers and sisters live in my heart. The conversations that I have with my remaining sister, Colleen, are about Polly's overall goodness!

So inspired . . . "Three Sisters."

Three Sisters

Memories recall the familiar bond
Knowing there's one who has gone beyond
We are two sisters left in a fold
Recalling one life that's often retold

We live our lives from day to day
With our sister's presence in all we say
When hearing a laugh that sounds like hers
We look that way when this occurs

She loved each moment and she was kind to all
And was so courageous when she took the fall
But sisters wonder what she would have been like
If she had remained to live out her life

But she believed in angels and accepted her fate
And knew that with God she had a date
Within the sky her star cast a powerful glow
And stays with us wherever we may go

She collected bells of every shape and sounds
With eye and ear searched small towns
She drove her car, on old dusty red dirt roads
To find temporary relief from her heavy loads

With smiles for strangers, each heart would lift
And she treasured each moment as a special gift
We hear church bells much to our delight
And know her faith has kept us right

Opossum's Thoughts Prelude

When I see all the opossums that are killed by seemingly unaware drivers, my heart feels sad, as they are the only marsupial in North America, and are unique. Opossums are nocturnal, and car lights blind them when crossing roads at night. They are slow moving; it is impossible for them to avoid the danger of cars. If drivers were more aware, I am sure they would want to make it safer for opossums, who go onto the roads to clean up the carcasses of the lost animals.

So inspired . . . "Opossum's Thoughts."

Opossum's Thoughts

We've been given a life that really stinks
God gave us the job of cleaning the streets
Did he take into consideration
The many unaware drivers we would meet
Because he did give us slow moving feet
Which makes crossing the road quite a feat
So please watch how you're driving
We need a big brake
For we could be carrying our babies
And all our lives are at stake

Our Good Buddy Prelude

My brother Don showed up one day at our house with a Maine coon cat. This small cat was abandoned and beaten when he appeared on Don's doorstep. The orphaned little one allowed Don to feed him, but he wouldn't let anyone else touch him. As Don's family already had a cat, he decided to bring the little cat to our farm where he could live in the barn.

We tried calling him various names, but he answered to none of them. My dad always called everyone "Buddy." One morning while Don and I were talking, the cat walked up and Don said, "Hey, Buddy." The cat started purring and seemed to approve of this name, so "Buddy" he became. He became part of our family and was loved and respected by all who met him.

The cat adjusted well to the busy barn life—tractors coming and going noisily, amid constant and varied activity. Being very clever and intelligent, the cat quickly trained the men to work around his schedule. He liked to eat on time, and tolerated no nonsense. The barn schedule was arranged to meet his needs.

Each morning he was in his spot, waiting for my nephew, Tony, who he preferred to feed him. When Tony's truck started up at his house over a mile away, Buddy knew he would soon be fed. The entire staff knew to watch Buddy's behavior to know when Tony would arrive. This cat was accurate. On the weekends he condescended to allow someone else to feed him. He came to the kitchen door or circled the house to find someone to feed him on time.

He liked to sleep by the radio. His music of choice was country, and he preferred George Strait. He became terribly upset if someone forgot this and changed the radio station.

Whenever I was tending the garden, he lingered close by, seemingly oblivious to my presence. However, when I moved to another area, I would find him again close by, always studiously ignoring my activity. He followed me around at a discreet distance whenever I walked or worked outside. I always felt that I had a guardian.

We were blessed with his companionship for almost fifteen years. He just left one morning. He had not been feeling well, so this was his decision. He left as he had lived—strictly on his own terms. We miss Buddy every day.

So inspired . . . "Our Good Buddy."

Our Good Buddy

The barn became Buddy's home
He quickly settled in
But he had a lot of injuries
And needed time to mend

The neighborhood felines
Carefully kept their distance
As he circled his yard
With soldierly insistence

He didn't purr "please"
As you prepared his eats
He just quietly waited
For his daily treats

As a hunter
He was the best
Mice, birds and butterflies
Could never stop and rest

He chose your company
In his own good time
With an attitude of
"Never you mind"

He decided to leave
As he had checked in
It was his decision
Right to the end

We will miss our Buddy
Our Maine coon cat
And will honor the spot
Where he always sat

When he arrives in cat heaven
He will claim a spot as his own
Saint Peter will welcome him
And know our good Buddy has arrived home

Skinny Tree Prelude

My great niece, Jessie, who was four years old at the time, was visiting me one day. We were in the backyard enjoying our time together.

She asked, "Do you know what 'pretend' means?"

"Sure," I responded.

I continued, "Do you want to play pretend?

"Yes, yes Aunt Jerry, you pretend first."

"Well," I said, "I will be a red tailed hawk and fly up to the top of the tallest white pine. What a view I will enjoy, and what fun I will have, swaying back and forth when the wind blows."

"Okay, okay, okay," she said, giggling. "Now me, I will be a skinny tree."

"Why a skinny tree?" I asked her.

"Because they don't get fat, they get taller and stronger, and they live a long, long time, and the birds will build nests on me," she said.

"Yes, my darling Jessie, I, the red tailed hawk, will light at the very top of the magnificent pine that is you, and I will never, ever fly by without a hello, or to tell you how much you are loved." A smile lit up her sweet little face.

"Okay, Aunt Jerry, okay."

So inspired . . . "Skinny Tree."

Skinny Tree

God looked down on the world
And saw, then spoke to, a precious, chubby little
girl

"Take a walk with ME in your mind
And a skinny tree you will surely find

Enjoy a walk each day with glee
Keep walking until you reach this tree

Get on your knees, and say a prayer:
'Please God, make me as skinny as this tree'

While walking each day, keep your joy for life,
And you won't need to ask me twice:

You'll be as skinny as this tree

This tree will grow to a majestic height
And you will live to be a lovely sight

With faithful walking everyday
This will be, precious one, you are under way

For, I bless you, and this beautiful tree
With all this walking, good health you'll see"

Big Brother Prelude

As we grew up on the farm, the wooded area near our house was our playground. Throughout the woods were trails, creeks, and ponds for crawfish catching, railroad tracks, and caves. Endless adventures awaited us everyday and fueled our imaginative minds.

Knowing that we had our fearless big brother Marvin to look out for us, we were always brave because we knew that he would always protect us. He never let us down.

My wish for all children is they could know the safety of having a big brother like mine. Marvin turned seventy five in February of 2007.

So inspired . . . "Big Brother."

Big Brother

Big brother built a rope swing
He shouted, while flying over rocky ravine
"Hey! Look at me, do it this way!"
We smile with joy, remembering that day

We grabbed hold, and took flight
Feeling like Tarzan of the movie reels
Copying our big brother without fear
While hanging on to that old tire wheel

Big brother led us whenever he could
On adventurous hikes deep in the woods
Fostering memories of wondrous childhood forays
Blazing trails of pretend, with big brother as Robin Hood

He dug cave dwellings
Into dark, scary red clay banks
We followed with pride swelling
Each according to our rank

Knife throwing was perfected
On the old cedar near the pond
Using knives he'd collected
From grandpa and uncles fond

He built fires for traipsing hobos
Camped beside the railroad tracks
We stole our mama's canned food
And hid it in big brother's backpack

Big brother cut firewood all day
We would watch in awe
As he wielded ax and saw
The chips flew and the woodpile grew

Mama often hollered
From the open kitchen door
"Marvin, pile the wood up high,
Stack those little one's arms up to the sky!"

Big brother made us feel safe
So we grew up with trust
We honor our big brother
Who helped shape our character for us

He built fires for traipsing hobos
Camped beside the railroad tracks
We stole our mama's canned food
And hid it in big brother's backpack

34

Blood Sucker Prelude

As a friend was helping me weed and deadhead in the flower garden, she received a nasty bite on her arm from a mosquito. She asked, "Do you know the purpose of a mosquito in the cycle of life?"

So inspired . . . "The Blood Sucker."

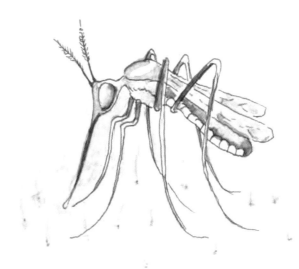

Blood Sucker

Whatever was God thinking when he made that dipterous bug,
Who invades your serene place and makes you come unplugged?
They buzz your ears and suck your blood;
Who needs them in the neighborhood?

Did it light upon God's arm and suck the red blood out?
Then fly into the world breeding millions all about?

Just when you get all settled and put your feet to rest,
Here it comes buzzing for a little blood fest.
We spray our bodies with Deet and don't let water stand.
Still they come around and invade Dixieland.

They carry the West Nile virus and malaria too.
Now a new surprise for us, here comes the Asian flu.
The birds are a dying, people and animals are getting ill,
And still no one can tell us why the mosquito came to kill.

I'm sure they have a purpose, while on this earth they dwell,
But I think we would all be happier, if God
Had them inject us with a nice zinfandel.

So tell us entomologist, whatever did God think,
When the mosquito came around for his first drink?

Micro Things Prelude

As a child I was fascinated with insects and the incredible architects that they are. I was especially intrigued with the very tiny insects that we so readily destroy just because, never questioning why. We destroy these tiny ones with little awareness of all the hard work that has gone into building their homes. We destroy them while they are carrying out the tasks that nature intends for them to do.

I was very impressed by an experience that my husband, Harry, told me about. There were a lot of stray cats in his neighborhood. Each night he put out food and milk for them. After setting the food out one night, he later checked and saw a snail eating what was left of the cat food. The next night when he checked the food, to his surprise the mama snail was back, with daddy snail and three babies in tow. They were coming up the steps to get their share of the food and milk.

This story changed the way I think about spraying any kind of poison in the garden. It all works out fine and my garden is full of interesting insects.

I have renewed respect for all the wonderful creatures of planet Earth, for their purposes in being here, and for the many varied contributions they make. They so rightly deserve this respect. We're all in this together.

So inspired . . . "Micro Things."

Micro Things

Micro things are all around
Working at their tasks
Whether in the air or on the ground
They are rarely there to bask.

Meticulously they build
A home you can destroy
By running and by playing
Or by just being a boy.

Watch where you are walking
A family is living there
You could destroy an anthill
That was built with detailed care.

Webs of writing spiders
With their hieroglyphics' art
Can withstand a hurricane
But not a human thrust.

So next time you take a walk
And put that big foot down
Always be aware
You could be tearing down a town.

The Walk for Health Prelude

My older brother, Marvin, had a near death experience when he suffered from a heart attack. He was air lifted to St. Joseph Hospital in Atlanta; the medics saved his life, after his heart stopped beating en route.

He survived and healed with a tremendous outpouring of love from his family, along with wonderful doctors and nurses. We were not ready to see him depart from the family circle.

The doctors attending Marvin were amazed at his recovery and commented that, if they were ever in ill health, they would want a family like Marvin's, one that would never give up for one second, and would fight alongside him for his life and return to good health.

After Marvin was released from the hospital, he was given health procedures to follow. One of these lifestyle changes was to take a walk each day. Truly committed to his recovery, Marvin walked faithfully. Invariably, each time he takes a walk some happenstance occurs and he returns with a new story to tell from the timeworn rocker on his front porch.

So inspired . . . "The Walk for Health."

The Walk for Health

Taking a walk can have meaning,
But sitting and rocking is where I'm leaning.
My doctor said, "Get out of that chair."
"Your heart's slowing down and you don't seem to care."

So, with new walking shoes, I started out early.
The fog rolled in and the sky looked pearly.
Striding down the road, I stumbled on a rock
And, what do you know, I took a big flop.

Keeping to my course, although somewhat shot,
I looked down at my ankle, but couldn't see past my pot.
My breath getting short, my heart beating fast,
Sweat coming down, but I hoped to last.

With swelling ankle, my health walk cut short,
I met my new neighbor, who was looking quite port.
"Where have you been?" he asked with a grin.
"Out for my health walk," I said, limping along.

"Stop by and visit," he said with a laugh.
"Come on, man, take a rest."
"Sitting on the porch is what we do best."
"No, kind sir, I must be on my way.
If I'm going to get fit, it starts this day."

Happy Day Prelude

In the morning, I often awaken to a view of the sunrise. My bedroom window is facing a lake, which has a small island with beech, dogwood and white pine trees on it. I can reach the island by a winding, moss covered footpath that runs alongside the lake to a Monet type of bridge, which connects the island to the path. Some of the beech trees on the island entwine toward the bridge.

With the sunlight of the new day shining on the white trunks of the beech trees, and with the lovely island reflecting in the water, I am blessed to have inspiration every morning.

I see each day as a chance to have a happy day.

So inspired . . . "Happy Day."

Happy Day

Say your prayers every night.
Question your day, wrong or right.
When we confess, God has his way,
And let's have a happy day.

Shedding Old Contentments Prelude

There are memories from my childhood that I have carried within my heart throughout my lifetime. I once read that each of us adds a little bit to our character, both good and bad, from every person we have ever met, ultimately contributing to the person that we become.

One person who has stayed with me, walking quietly through those memories, is a neighbor who lived next door. From early childhood until my family moved away during my teen years, I saw Cassie every day. She was always working in her beautiful gardens, painting fences or outhouses, minding her chickens, cooking, or doing any of the thousands of mundane things that make the substance of our lives.

Even if Cassie got upset when the neighborhood children ran through her garden or played childish pranks on her, she always held an equitable, calm demeanor. I was captivated by her. I frequently went out my way to speak to her or "cut across" her property, hoping for an invitation into her life, if only for a short moment. I liked her. In later years as a teen, I felt honored to be able to do some special favors for her.

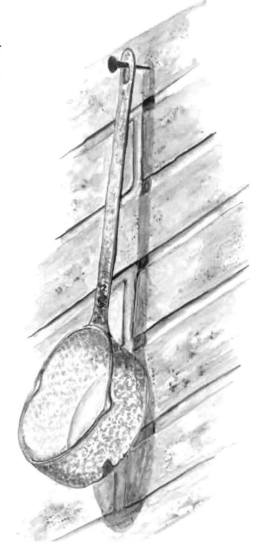

Our home, in contrast with Cassie's well ordered world, was in a constant uproar—loud and chaotic. With mama hollering at us six children, animals everywhere, constant rivalry among our siblings, everyone doing the chores of a large family, getting our schoolwork done and, of course, our daily adventures into the woods, our home was always in high gear. Even the evenings were hectic with baths on the back porch, amid fights as to whose turn it was to have the first bath. This prized position of "first bath" status was very sought after. With the bath water both getting cooler and carrying the previous bathers' contributions, being at the end of the line of six active kids was not a great joy.

Cassie's enchanting and tranquil home seemed to be everything that our home was not. She lived in a charming, picture perfect white house with a white picket fence that encircled the front yard. The yard was continually swept clean with a handmade brush broom. These brooms were made by gathering scrubby bushes, then cutting each branch to varying lengths from three to five feet, and binding the branches together to form a handle. These brooms left nothing to their wake. Cassie would tolerate neither leaf, nor a single blade of grass in her yard. From the constant sweeping, the yard stayed as pristine and sandy white as a sugar beach.

Cassie carried her perfection through all that existed on her property. The chicken house was painted a rich forest green, and was cleaned each day. The chicken litter was put into tin buckets, which were then neatly lined up along the barn shelter until the litter could be disposed of. The barn shelter also housed firewood in neat, symmetrical stacks.

Two sky blue rockers sat alone on the front porch. Only the occasional breezes would set them rocking. The deep well in the back yard was covered by an arbor. The arbor, in turn, was covered with yellow roses from a running rose bush. The arbor seemed to be made entirely of the lovely, fragrant blooms. Indeed, tendrils from the bush continued their journey up into the oak tree nearby. A blue speckled enamel dipper hung on a large red nail beside the well. The freshly drawn water was always ice cold, and was a refreshing treat any time.

Cassie's home was a magical place. Yet, with all the careful perfection that she had created around her, I never saw Cassie smile. I never heard her laugh out loud, not even once.

Cassie baked incredible lemon pies. Her back porch was just off the kitchen, with wood shutters that opened outward. She would line lemon pies, freshly baked and piled high with meringue, along the open shuttered ledge to cool. The sweet scent of those pies was sheer heaven. Once in a blue moon, she would tell us to stop by after Sunday service for a piece of pie. We could scarcely wait; needless to say, we knew that heaven would be waiting for us. When we finally got to

that first tart sweet bite, the crust still slightly warm, we felt that God excused Cassie from having to attend church. The gift of those amazing pies must surely have given her special grace. We would "cut across" Cassie's back yard every week, with the excuse that we could get to Sunday sermon a bit quicker that way. Often, Cassie would greet us at the well, line us up in the stair step order, and pin yellow rosebuds on our clothes. After dispatching us in style, she would take a stroll. Dressed in her usual cotton dress—faded and dull, but always clean and starched—she always walked in the same direction, always at the same time and at the same pace.

This ritual Sunday morning stroll may have been her way of observing her faith, without the formality of going to Sunday sermons. However, one Sunday morning, a wondrous happening took place at our little white church.

So inspired . . . "Shedding Old Contentments."

Shedding Old Contentments

Cassie was weary from the same lonely strolls.
A change in direction would be song for her soul.
She'd have a jaunty new walk, a sassy silk Sunday dress,
And a new, over large, charming, pricey straw hat.

The little white church would be a good place to start,
To find new inspiration for her troubled heart.
The parishioners would surely stare when she walked in—
For this would be her very first time to attend.

Humming as she strolled, she walked alone,
But, in her ear, she kept hearing a whistling tone.
A strapping whippoorwill was following along.
He lit on her straw hat, and started singing her song.

With her longing soul, a winged friend just might
Want to share in her journey, to surprise and delight.
As the church bells rang in a welcoming sound,
Cassie and her whippoorwill were bound to astound.

47

The church doors opened wide to welcome all in.
Two mysterious new friends waited for church to begin,
With his white tail feathers, and strong white bill,
He was perched on Cassie's hat—her new friend, the whippoorwill.

Cassie and the whippoorwill were about to sit down,
When the organist started to play—t'was a heavenly sound.
Cassie began to sing in a wondrous voice.
Her back up singer was her bird of choice,

The parishioners listened; their voices were soundless.
They laid their hymnals down, most intently, with politeness.
When Cassie and her whippoorwill were finished with their song,
The two rose to depart, and then, quickly, they were gone.

Remembering the day she left old contentments behind,
When the people were kind, and of generous minds—
When Cassie changed direction, if only for one day,
She made a winged friend, and found a friendship that would stay.

Harry and Zabo taken at Lake Tahoe in 1954.
Harry is in white trunks and Zabo is in black trunks.

The Man Who Owns Nothing Prelude

I finally met Harry's special, dear friend, Zabo. Their friendship has been continuous for fifty years. I had heard countless wonderful stories about this friend's kindness, his and Harry's travels along with fellow body builders, when they were performing with the Mae West Show, and many other adventures.

When I met Zabo, he was already in his seventies. I was not disappointed. We have been delighted to have him visit us on numerous occasions. On his most recent visit to celebrate his eightieth birthday, I found him still sharp, handsome, and the nicest of men. He is a follower of Buddhism and a voracious reader.

One of our many conversations led to a discussion about people accumulating too many possessions. Zabo said, "I don't have that worry. I own nothing."

So inspired . . . "The Man Who Owns Nothing."

The Man Who Owns Nothing

For this old time bodybuilder
With a past of flexing and competing
Reaching eighty is a milestone
Now retirement and well being

Still a handsome man
Who had women galore
He loved them and left them
With memories to store

A loyal friend
The best of his kind
Will give you his shirt
And never mind

He has lived his life
In his own laidback way
Earning just enough money
For wine, books and play

And not having possessions
Doesn't give him anxiety
He loves reading and friends
And a peaceful society

The beach is a must
With close friends he can trust

The sand and the sun
Are always close by
He will not move north
So his kids don't try

His lined face has aged well
From the sun and a tan
We are blessed to know this re-
freshing, novel man

He is blessed with children
Who love their dad
A satisfying family life
He could have had

He believes in Buddhism
And lives his life meager
Meditates with incense
And remains the intriguer

Living eighty years of life
Singing his own song
The man who owns nothing
Hasn't lived his life wrong

When the Barker Came to Call Prelude

The Barkers, our neighbors in King Mountain, North Carolina, had a most special dog, a golden retriever named Beauregard Bodacious. The Barkers worked, so Beau was home alone during the day. He often sat at the curb or curled up in front of a huge stone at the entrance to our neighbor Tom's driveway, waiting for a car to come up the mountain. He would follow you to your door and bark his greeting for you to come out and play.

Beau passed away in December 2002. Everyone on the mountain felt that we had lost a special friend. Tom had a special memorial carved into the stone where Beau had sat so often, watching for a friend.

Beau spent many hours helping me in my gardens. Every stick I threw away, Beau brought back. I miss his beautiful spirit.

So Inspired . . . "When the Barker Came to Call."

When the Barker Came to Call

Heading for the Highlands
Feeling very blessed,
We climb the winding roads
Seeking long awaited rest

Unpack the car, winding down,
Waiting for the "Barker" to come around

But where is our cheerful greeting?
The Barker always comes to call—
He stands barking at our back door
If we don't respond at all

We miss our fine and faithful friend
When summer comes to call
We wonder who will greet us
Among the mists of fall

But I smile when I think of Beau
Running to the pearly gate
Barking loud and persistent,
Hoping he's not late

Saint Peter will fall in love
When he sees that happy face,
Beau will greet the new arrivals
With nobility and grace

He will perform his happy dance
As he did for one and all
We will miss him on the mountain
And remember when the Barker came to call.

GB's Place Prelude

I grew up just outside a small town of Smyrna, Georgia. Smyrna was a typical southern town. Everyone knew you and your business, and they didn't mind reprimanding someone else's kids if the kids got out of line. You always felt that your neighbors were watching out for you. You felt safe.

There were no fast food restaurants, but there was a wonderful diner called GB's Place right next to the railroad tracks. A big treat for me was when I had enough coins to buy a burger at GB's. This was no billions served, cookie cutter fast food, but the best hamburger on planet Earth, made especially for me by GB himself. I can still taste the culinary perfection of those burgers. I felt so special ordering one.

So inspired . . . "GB's Place."

GB's Place

Memories come and rest in my mind
Of a place that sat by the railroad tracks
It was filled with laughter and small town talk
And kids hopscotched on the front sidewalk

GB was the owner, a rare man indeed
He didn't run his place on profit and greed
Rules and regulations were not posted on the door
Everyone felt welcome and nobody cared what you wore

We sat at a counter of shiny Formica red
On sunny yellow stools, while waiting to be fed
The aroma of the burgers came drifting out
GB knew the kids' orders; he gave us first clout

His kind voice would ring out from the back
"Your burgers, kids, will be right out. How's your Pa and Uncle Mac?"
"No drinks today," knowing we couldn't pay
"This one's on me, it's your lucky day"

Each time we ate our juicy burgers so grand
We smiled with contentment because of a special man
We only knew his name, and the kindness he gave
To a bunch of country kids, in our hearts GB has stayed

Going back to our town where GB's place stood
The same railroad tracks still serve the neighborhood
Kids can buy burgers, at a fast food place
But, they will never know the joy
Of seeing GB's smiling kind face

Footnote:
G. B. Williams owned and operated GB's Place from 1937 to 1974
Painting inspired from a photograph
With special thanks to the Smyrna Historical Society

Secondhand Yellow Raincoat Prelude

Growing up in a large family in the rural south, we rarely got new clothes. We wore hand me downs from relatives and friends, as did everyone we knew back then. Our big brother, Marvin, started working odd jobs, and people sometimes gave him their secondhand clothes. One time he brought home an old, patent yellow fireman's coat that he gave to our little brother Don.

As the youngest child, Don spent lots of time by himself. As a result, he developed a keen sense of imagination—an old tire was a truck, a stick was a stallion to ride while chasing villains away from his make believe town.

He loved that secondhand raincoat. He wore it night and day, playing fireman, saving the citizens of his imaginary town, and for countless other adventures.

So inspired . . . "Secondhand Yellow Raincoat."

Secondhand Yellow Raincoat

Big brother brought home
An old fireman's coat
He gave it to little brother
Who loved it so

This beautiful little boy
With eyes of chocolate brown
Wore a patent yellow raincoat
In his make believe town

A golden skin castle-building boy
Who lived in dreams of little doubt
Running with laughter, singing out
On fast bare feet he bobbed about

We saw that flash of yellow
Coming around the bend
He drove his pretend fire truck
With his imaginary friends

His truck was an old tire
His coat was secondhand
But he put out every fire
In his make believe land

He was the coolest bravest sheriff
The outlaws left his town
For the boy in the yellow raincoat
Was there to bring the bad guys down

His white horse was a hickory stick
Sitting high in the saddle with pride
The citizens slept safe at night
With their brave sheriff on his ride

He outgrew the yellow raincoat
But carries memories that run deep
For the qualities that his raincoat gave
Were qualities he could keep

My brother developed manly ways
Moved on to grown up strife
But still remembers those carefree days
Of a very happy life

57

The Samples Prelude

Our beautiful, local market gives away all kinds of samples. When I shop there, I love to watch the customers as they try new products. Sometimes, as with one product in particular, this is quite comical to see.

So inspired . . . "The Samples."

The Samples

When walking through the market
It was busy as can be
I came upon some green juice
Take samples; they are free

A line was gathered there
And I watched shoppers lift their cups
And with just a bit of caution
They take a generous sup

Their faces became distorted
As the green juice all went down
On its pathway to the stomach
For digestion to come around

The shoppers walked a little further
Until free cookies came in view
And with smiles upon their faces
They sampled one or two

I watched their happy faces
That's what a chocolate chip will do
So why is this green juice
So very good for you?

Aunt Jerry's Magic Quilt Prelude

A good friend gave me an antique quilt at a time in my life when I needed comfort. I kept that quilt for thirty years.

My great-niece Katie called one night. She said she was having nightmares and was afraid to go to sleep. I felt it was time to pass the quilt on to another who needed it.

The quilt has worked its magic again. How lovely to be able to pass on a magical quilt and comfort a child.

So inspired . . . "Aunt Jerry's Magic Quilt."

Aunt Jerry's Magic Quilt

A magic quilt, so it's been told,
Was sent to Katie to treasure as gold.
Aunt Jerry said, "Katie, at the end of day
Just listen, and you'll hear it say."

"When day is done and your mind is full
Of life's rich lessons and a little bull,
Just kneel beside me for your prayers
And you will sleep with no nightmares."

"Think of all the hands that stitched my seams,
Adding love and energy for starlight dreams.
I will cover you throughout the night,
As you are sleeping, tucked in tight."

"Then rest your head upon my threads,
And nothing else need be said.
I'll stay with you and watch you grow,
Bringing wonderful memories in our tow."

"So cover up—stay nice and warm.
I'm right here, all soft and worn.
When morning breaks another day,
Within your soul sweet peace will stay."

Within Wood Prelude

Since early childhood, I have had a close connection with trees. They have provided my life with memories that have helped shape my character, and with stories to pass on to the next generation. With so many gifts from trees, I started thinking how these living treasures have affected our lives.

When I was a child, my mama taught me how to cook extraordinary meals on a wood-fueled, iron and white, glossy enamel cook stove that always held delectable food. A side warmer stored left over biscuits and teacakes. The coffee pot and teakettle were ready for a warm drink when we came in from the cold.

As children, my sister and I spent many hours in an enchanting playhouse we built between the roots of a big oak tree. Parts of its roots were about four to six inches above the ground and fanned out like giant octopus tentacles. We filled these spaces with salvaged treasures from the dump behind our house next to the railroad tracks. The trips to the dump were an adventure we looked forward to, especially since our mama had forbidden us to go anywhere near the railroad tracks.

The great oaks in our yard were also a gathering place for family reunions, games of knife throwing, hopscotch, jump rope, and shows that were put on with neighboring kids. They sheltered us from the hot Georgia sun while we took lazy afternoon naps. I understand why the mighty oak is called "the king of trees."

Cedars and pine trees were our choices for Christmas. Looking for the trees was always a wonderful adventure for us kids. Daddy would take us into the woods to find this select tree. By the time each kid voiced an opinion on which tree we would be taking home, we had stretched our adventure into an all day outing. In the end though, daddy made the final decision.

Mostly, fallen trees provided the family with wood for the fireplaces that were our only source of heat. We spent many wonderful family get togethers, in front of the fireplaces. Daddy and our older brother cut all this firewood, and the younger children carried it inside to a big wood box in the canning room.

Every tree's parts were put to good use. The chips were used in the barn animals' stalls and pens. Daddy made slingshots out of branches for us to play with, and the small pieces were used as starter wood for the fireplaces.

Plum trees surrounded the wheat fields, and a big mulberry tree stood in an open field all alone. All provided us with great jams, jellies and mulberry layer cake that sent our mouths to watering with just the thought of it.

A giant oak in the backyard carried a thrill ride; we called it "the shoot to shoot." A cable was attached to the oak. The cable ran down a hill, which helped us gather speed, then we were sent on a ride of our lives: over the horse and cow grazing pasture, continuing over a spring that wound through a red clay, six to eight foot ditch, and landing us on a flat, softly-dug place piled with leaves and straw to cushion our landing.

We held on for our lives to a carved, smooth piece of wood that was attached to a roller from the cable. After the very first ride, this was after our big brother decided we were old enough, he carved our ID into the stick, a proud moment. We felt brave and no longer a little kid. We got a good grip, lifted our feet off the ground and off we soared. When we finally touched down, the one thing on our minds was not that we had landed safely, but rather how quickly we could walk back to the starting place and do it again. The marvelous memories we have of trees we will carry forever, and the next generation will continue to pass them on. I give thanks for all the fantastic gifts trees have brought into our lives and will continue to do so.

So inspired . . . "Within Wood."

Within Wood

Within that acorn
There is a tree
To house a swing
For you and me.

Within wood,
A summer place
Where families gather
And kids give chase.

Within wood,
A door does open
To let us in
With friendly words spoken.

Within wood,
A table stands
With friends around
Holding hands.

Within wood
A chair resides
To rest someone's
Broad backside.

Within wood
Are salad forks
To mix your greens
And eat and sort.

Within wood,
There is a bed
To rest your head
After prayers are said.

Within wood,
A cabinet's built
To store Grandma's
Antique quilts.

Within wood
A cradle rocks
To soothe a baby
'Til crying stops.

Within wood,
A spinning wheel
To spin the cloth
That binds and shields.

Within wood,
An arbor stands
To guide the vine
From earth and sand.

Within wood,
A garden bench
To sit and ponder
What's over yonder.

Within wood,
A tree will fall
And house the animals
Big and small.

Within wood,
Termites dine
And tell their friends
To bring the wine.

Within wood,
A dugout glides
To move a family
That has no ride.

Within wood,
A roller rink
So kids may skate
And flirt and wink.

Within wood,
A pole's installed
To carry a message
For your phone call.

Within wood,
A stage floor shines
With Broadway shows
And pantomime.

Within wood,
Drumsticks beat—
A marching band
With many feet.

Within wood,
A baby grand
To compose a tune
For a swing band.

Within wood,
A walking stick
To support your grandpa
When he's sick.

Within wood,
A window opens
To see the world
With views unbroken.

Within wood,
A barn stands tall
While horses rest
Within their stalls.

Within wood,
Are wagon parts
That opened new frontiers
For solid starts.

Within wood,
The white pine stands
For early settlers
To build the land.

Within wood,
Charcoal's made
By a frontier family
For warmth and trade.

Within wood,
A fence arrives
To protect or divide
That's for you to decide.

Within wood,
Bridges span
To connect new neighbors
With helping hands.

Within wood,
Pine chips are plenty
To landscape gardens
Outside the city.

Within wood,
A box is made
To hold one's jewels—
Rubies and jade.

Within wood,
An altar is built
Where people kneel
And confess their guilt.

Within wood,
A pine box waits.
You live your life
And then it takes.

Within wood,
A special pencil
To write my poems
For your attention.

Metamorphosed Prelude

While I was scanning a magazine one day, I came upon a short story about a delightful couple. They had bought an unremarkable beige house. Both being artists, they transformed the house into a wonderful work of art. So inspired . . . "Metamorphosed."

Metamorphosed

There once sat a dull beige house
With no laughter or beauty coming out
Then along came an artful pair
Who brought living magic with flair

They painted with red, green, and blues
Added trim of lattice and bamboo
Now vibrant this whimsical house is dull no more

A dull beige house metamorphosed with sass
You'll smile with delight if you wander past
A unique couple used their talent and heart
And gave a dull beige house a brand new start

Payback Prelude

I have read that squirrels learn by imitating other squirrels. They learn quickly that no one welcomes them at the bird feeders. People yell, put up special barriers, grease the poles, and in all manners contrive to defeat the squirrels. However the squirrels always seem to outsmart them.

One of my neighbors, who is not very nice to squirrels, is always having problems with squirrels doing mischievous things. I have found that, when I put nuts out, the squirrels stay busy gathering and storing, even though they do not hibernate; they eat lots of food to get their fur nice and thick for the cold weather.

As I fill the bird feeders and see the squirrels watching me, I can't help but wonder what they think of us humans.

So inspired . . . "Payback."

Payback

Squirrels may ponder their bad deeds
Then scrounge about and steal birdseeds
The birds don't care; they're willing to share
But man still says, "Don't you dare."

Squirrels approach with such care
They look around for extra fare
Man runs out and hollers and rants
And off squirrels run, then sit and chant

"Who are these crazies?" Squirrels do ask
"They put out food, then feel aghast."
"But our justice comes in small bites."
An electric wire and out go your house lights

A repairman is called, to correct the fault
It's those damn squirrels, they must be caught
Grey, red or black they are causing havoc all about
It will cost you plenty, have no doubt

Today the feeders get extra nuts, eat up squirrels, have your fill
For who can afford the repairman's bill?
So squirrels may revel in this good deed
And even leave leftover seed

Bask in the show, squirrels are fun to view
But just remember, they are watching you

Resting Pots Prelude

It was a beautiful, warm, sunny winter day when a friend stopped by to wish me a Happy New Year. I asked if she would like to take a walk through the gardens. She replied, "I'll return in the spring when all the flowers are in full bloom." I said, "Let's walk now when the gardens and pots are at rest, you will be surprised at all the fascinating happenings we will see, that one does not observe when the majestic show of the blooming flowers are in full bloom."

As my now curious friend and I walked and talked that day, I pointed out that each resting pot evokes a memory, and beauty is there to bring forth. A squirrel was busy hiding an acorn or a black walnut in one of the resting pots. Sometimes I am blessed and an absent-minded squirrel forgets where he hid his stash and a sprout will spring forth. I receive great pleasure of replanting them and often gift them to friends. As we continued our conversation, she began to ask questions about the different stages of the garden.

So inspired . . . "Resting Pots."

Resting Pots

Pots of all shapes and sizes sit in repose
They have earned a rest at summer's close
Flowers of red, purples and golds
That flourished, in the pots now decompose

The terra cotta pots will move inside
Because real harsh weather they can't abide
Glazed and concrete can tough it out
And will shine in springtime have little doubt

Delightful window boxes are left intact
A place for squirrels to hide winter snacks
A mighty oak seedling may break through
One of God's phenomenons for us to view

I like to see them taking a rest
Without the worry of summer's pests
They will wait for the elements to be right
Then rich soil will create a heavenly sight

My Bluebird Flight Prelude

A custom in the South with most large families is the older children take care of the younger ones. My younger brother Carl was often in my care. Carl was a beautiful child with golden hair and an adorable, sweet face with sky blue eyes and unique expressions.

One time, while Carl was in my care, I was weeding the garden. I noticed he was staring at something. He was about four years old at the time. When I asked what he was looking at, he pointed to a fence post and said, "A piece of sky is in my eye." Upon a closer look, I saw a bluebird checking out the cavity in the fence post. The hoeing was put aside as we sat and watched the beautiful bluebird build a nest.

So inspired . . . "My Bluebird Flight."

My Bluebird Flight

In my imagination I see myself as
A bluebird flying free

A piece of sky flying by
Lit on a fence post
In my eye

The bluebirds welcome me with flair
To share food they had gleaned
With particular care

"Wiggly worms, a grasshopper or two
Is the fare we've gathered
For lunch with you."

With slight trepidation
But not wishing to be rude
I take a crunchy bite, and finish my food

Enjoying their hospitality
Within the fence post nest
I give thanks for being their houseguest

My spirit is lifted, far beyond words
A far-reaching daydream made unique
By the mountain bluebirds

The bluebirds chirped in their local speech
Discussing my departure
Before darkness and I meet

"Our spirit will protect you
And guide you safely home
We value your graciousness and bid you shalom."

"I remember that day as a bluebird I lived
And look back with longing
When they light on my window sill."

A soft tingle of moisture
Landed on my shoulder simon pure
A bluebird's tear of delicate azure

With honor I shoulder each day of my life
A bluebird's tattoo, a reminder of my day in flight

Solo Prelude

I've always enjoyed morning walks and being alone with all of the beautiful creatures that inhabit the woods and lakes. One morning, while walking beside a small, muddy pond that borders the property, I heard a loud quacking. Upon closer investigation, I saw a big, beautiful white duck with a bright orange bill swimming alone in the pond, making perfect figure eights. I felt he was trying to impress me.

I was dazzled by this magnificent creature and looked forward to seeing him each morning on my walk. I named him "Solo."

Each day I would take seeds for a snack, letting him know he had a friend and that he was welcome. Solo was a delightful sight to me every day. He took up residence on the lake, which was closer to my home than the little pond. He was the king of the lake. It was a terribly sad day for me when he left.

I often felt that he kept moving from lake to lake, giving joy to other families. I think of him providing protection for other lake fowl that need him. I miss him dearly.

So inspired . . . "Solo."

Solo

"A little before sunrise,
I took a silent walk,
Listening to the soft sounds
And hearing nature's sweet talk

Breaking this silence
From a muddy old hole,
Came a forceful quacking
Such a sight to behold

A majestic white duck
Was swimming around,
And making a noisy,
But happy sound

He had a bright orange bill
And a friendly waddling way,
So I tossed him my trail mix
To entice him to stay

As I walked away,
His quaking got stronger.
"I'm so sorry, Solo
I can't stay any longer."

I looked out my window
At the break of day
I spotted Solo on the lake
Making figure eights his way

Solo cared for all the babies
Of the fallen geese
This majestic white duck
Was only there to please

As he is crossing the lake
Leaving a big wake behind
With all the orphan goslings
Following in a marching line

But this morning, the lake was quiet
His quacking I wanted to hear
I called out for Solo
But he did not appear

I searched near and far,
Up and down the lake,
Not a feather did I find,
Every effort did I make

God protect Solo
And find him a home
Such a special duck
Should never be alone

I still miss the beautiful Solo
With feathers white as snow
And with a heart so big
Surely angel wings he'll grow

So when I see a snow white duck,
With snow white angel wings,
That will be my Solo
And, oh, my heart will sing!

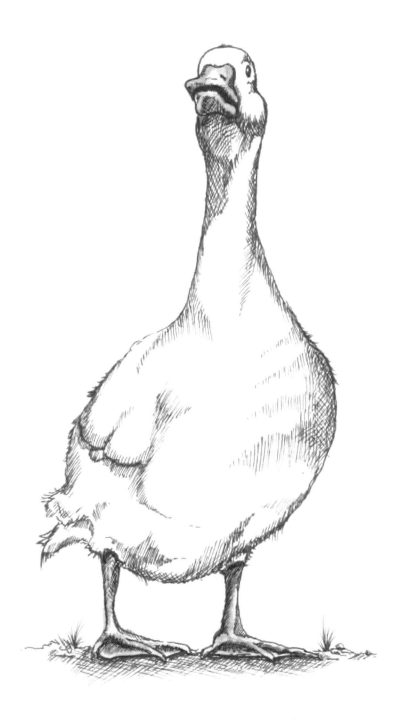

Passenger's Side Prelude

As my husband and I left for a short outing, he asked, "Would you like to drive?"
"No," I said, "I like to ride on the passenger's side."
So inspired . . . "Passenger's Side."

Passenger's Side

I think that
When taking a Sunday ride
It's better to sit on the passenger's side

You can relax, enjoy the view
And take life in stride
It's a joy, just to be
On the passenger's side

You can read a book
A cup of coffee in hand
Slip in a CD
And listen to a jazz band

Oh! Life is grand
On the passenger's side

You can take delight in
The pleasure of two
And you don't have to check
What's in the rearview

Put your seat back
Make an adjustment or two
Close your eyes softly
Enjoy the ride, as if it's your due

Sitting in the back seat
Can feel somewhat second class
Unless your driver is a chauffeur
Then your ride becomes first class

Me, I'll take the passenger's side
The reward is so much more
I love the ride—long or short
Just bring me safely to my door

So Inspired: Preludes and Poems is a heartwarming poetry collection that celebrates the sweetness of life. Through reflections of enriching personal experiences, Jerry Brown Schwartz inspires her readers to take in each passing moment and to focus on life's simple treasures.

Reflecting on her fulfilling life, Jerry Brown Schwartz composes her memories into words with simplicity and warmth. Each poem, filled with the concepts of love, kindness, and gratitude for the many joys of life, is complimented by a prelude that peers into this poet's soul.

You, the reader, are invited to discover the extraordinary within the mundane. Perhaps you will find inspiration within these pages to wish upon a falling star, protect all creatures great and small, and truly appreciate the gifts of the earth.